Smart, Clean Pigs

By Allan Fow...

Consultants:

Robert L. Hillerich, Ph.D., Bowling Green
State University, Bowling Green, Ohio

Mary Nalbandian, Director of Science,
Chicago Public Schools, Chicago, Illinois

Fay Robinson, Child Development Specialist

CHILDRENS PRESS®
CHICAGO

Design by Beth Herman Design Associates

Library of Congress Cataloging-in-Publication Data

Fowler, Allan
 Smart, clean pigs / by Allan Fowler.
  p. cm. –(Rookie read-about science)
 Summary: Briefly describes where pigs live, what they look like, and
how they behave.
 ISBN 0-516-06013-9
 1. Swine–Juvenile literature. [1. Pigs.] I. Title
 II. Series: Fowler, Allan. Rookie read-about science.
SF395.5.F69 1993
636.4–dc20   92-36365
               CIP
               AC

Smart, clean pigs?

4

Do you think pigs are dirty? And not very smart?

Many people think so — but that's because they don't know pigs.

If you ask anyone who takes care of pigs, he or she will probably tell you this:

Pigs are among the cleanest
and smartest animals.

Yes, pigs do roll around
in the mud – but for
a good reason.

9

All animals, including humans, need to sweat.

If you didn't sweat, you would feel much too hot in warm weather. Sweat helps your body cool off.

Pigs hardly sweat at all.

So how do they keep from getting too hot?

If a pig doesn't have
a pond or a tub of cold
water to cool off in,
it will use the next best
thing – mud.

In fact, pigs are the smartest of all farm animals.

Some people even keep
pigs as pets. Pigs can learn
many clever tricks.

Pigs are sometimes
called hogs or swine.

Sometimes a person is said to "eat like a pig."

That means he or she eats too much.

Well, pigs do eat a lot.
But they are too smart
to overeat.

They eat only as much
as they need to grow.
And they grow very big.

Baby pigs, called piglets, gain more than 200 pounds in their first six months.

And they keep growing!

Female pigs, called sows, weigh about 400 pounds when they are full grown.

Full-grown male pigs, called boars, can weigh more than 600 pounds.

On a farm, the pig's home
is called a pen or a sty.

A sow gives birth to a litter of six to twelve piglets.

A litter of playful piglets is fun to see at feeding time.

Watch them climb over
each other.

With their curly tails...
their flat-in-front snouts...
and their squeals and grunts...
piglets are cute and lovable.

But don't forget – they will soon grow up to be smart and clean.

And very, very big.

Words You Know

pigs

hogs   swine

snout

mud

litter of piglets   sow

boar

pen /sty

31

Index

About the Author

Allan Fowler is a free-lance writer with a background in advertising. Born in New York, he lives in Chicago now and enjoys traveling.

Photo Credits

Courtesy of Illinois State Fair – 23, 29, 31 (bottom left)

PhotoEdit – ©David Young-Wolff, 10; ©Elena Rooraid, 14; ©Mark Richards,15; ©Tony Freeman, 16

SuperStock International, Inc. – 26, 28; ©Garneau/Prevost, Cover; Pierre Ramaekers, 4, 25; ©Alvis Upitis, 6; ©Schuster, 7, 20; ©C.M. Slade, 12; ©Jerry Amster, 13; ©L. Willinger, 18; ©Sal Maimone, 19; ©Karl Kummels, 24

Valan – ©Harold V. Green, 9, 30 (bottom right); ©Francis Lepine, 21; ©Herman H. Geithoorn, 22

COVER: Pigs

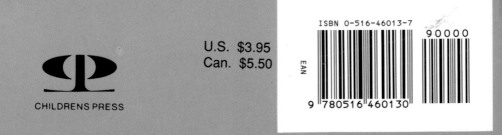

CHILDRENS PRESS

U.S. $3.95
Can. $5.50

ISBN 0-516-46013-7

EAN

9 780516 460130

90000